Manga Drawing Books How To Draw Action Manga Poses [B/W]

Learn Japanese Manga Eyes and Pretty Manga Face

By Gala Publication

Published by:

Gala Publication

ISBN-13: 978- 1508697107
ISBN-10: 1508697108

ⒸCopyright 2015 – Gala Publication

Table Of Content :

Step1

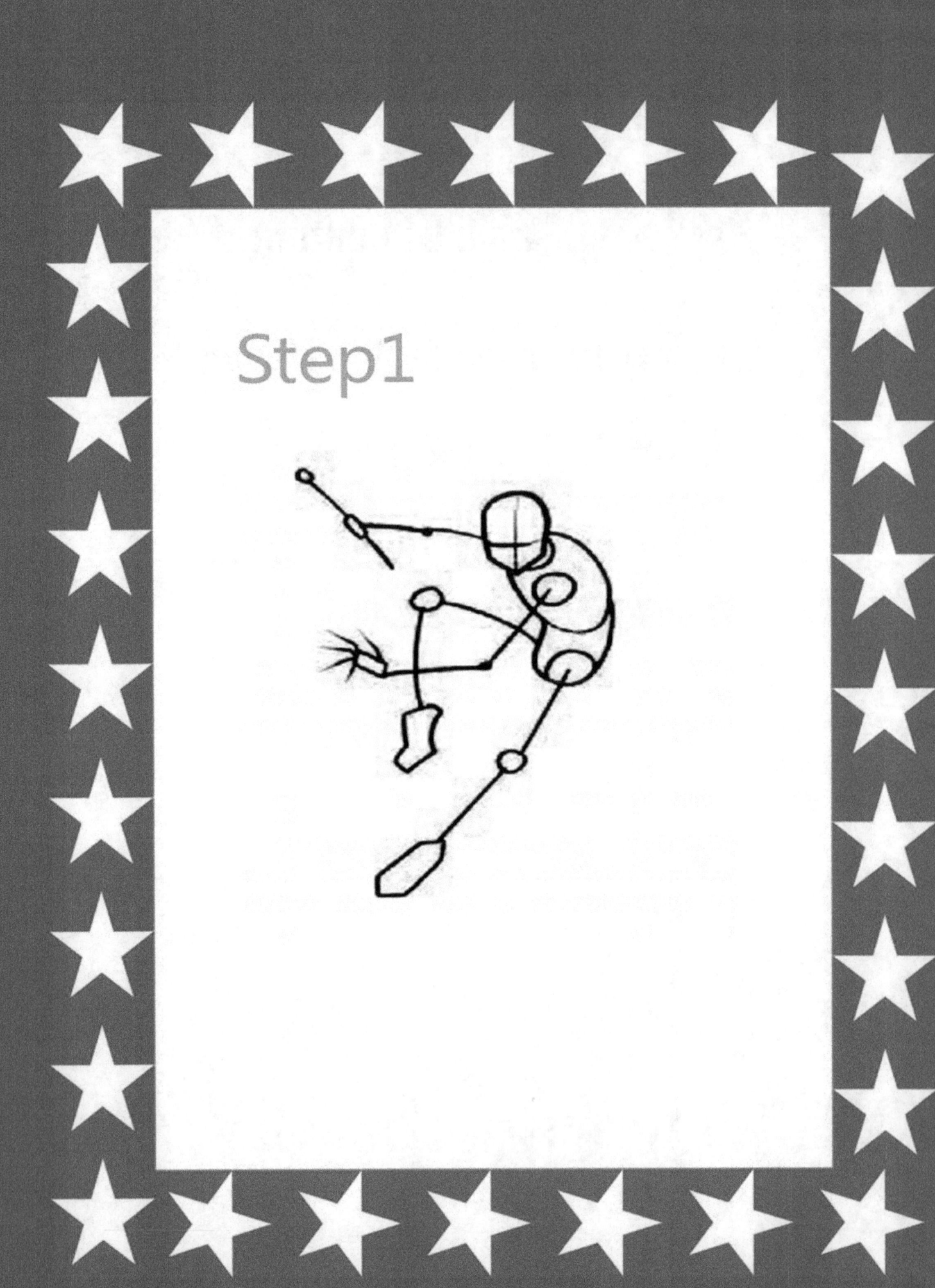

Step 2

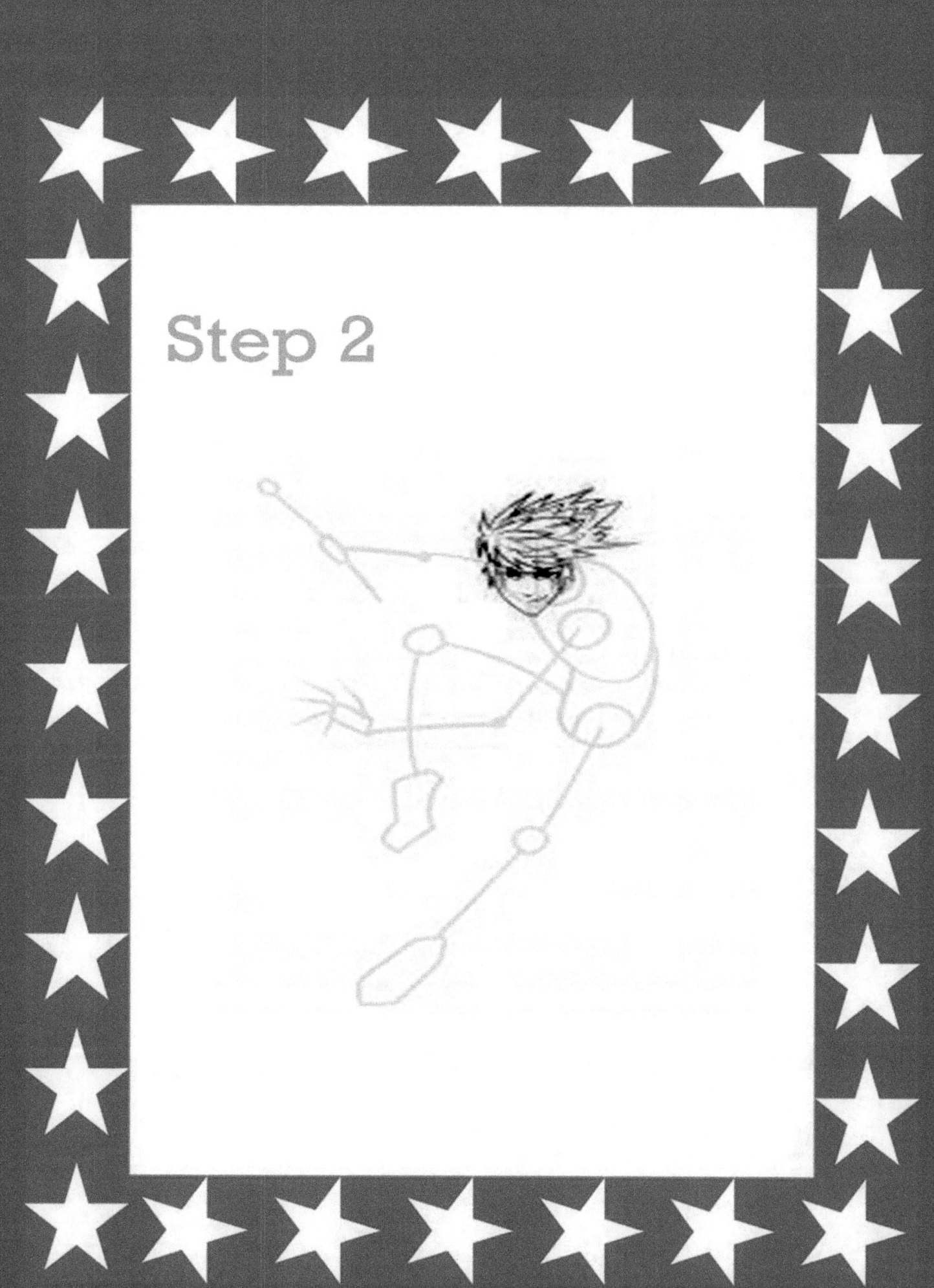

Step 3

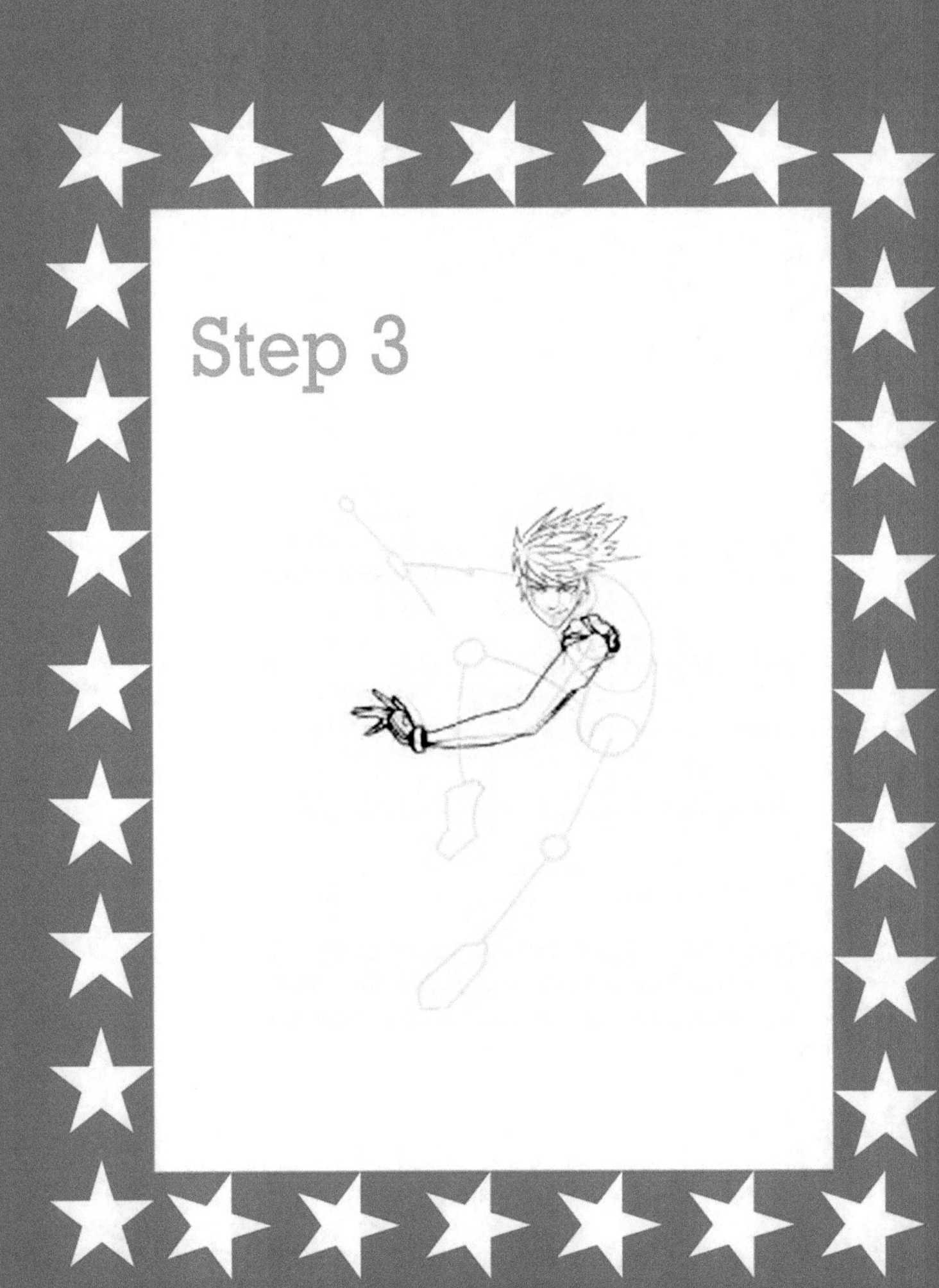

Step 4

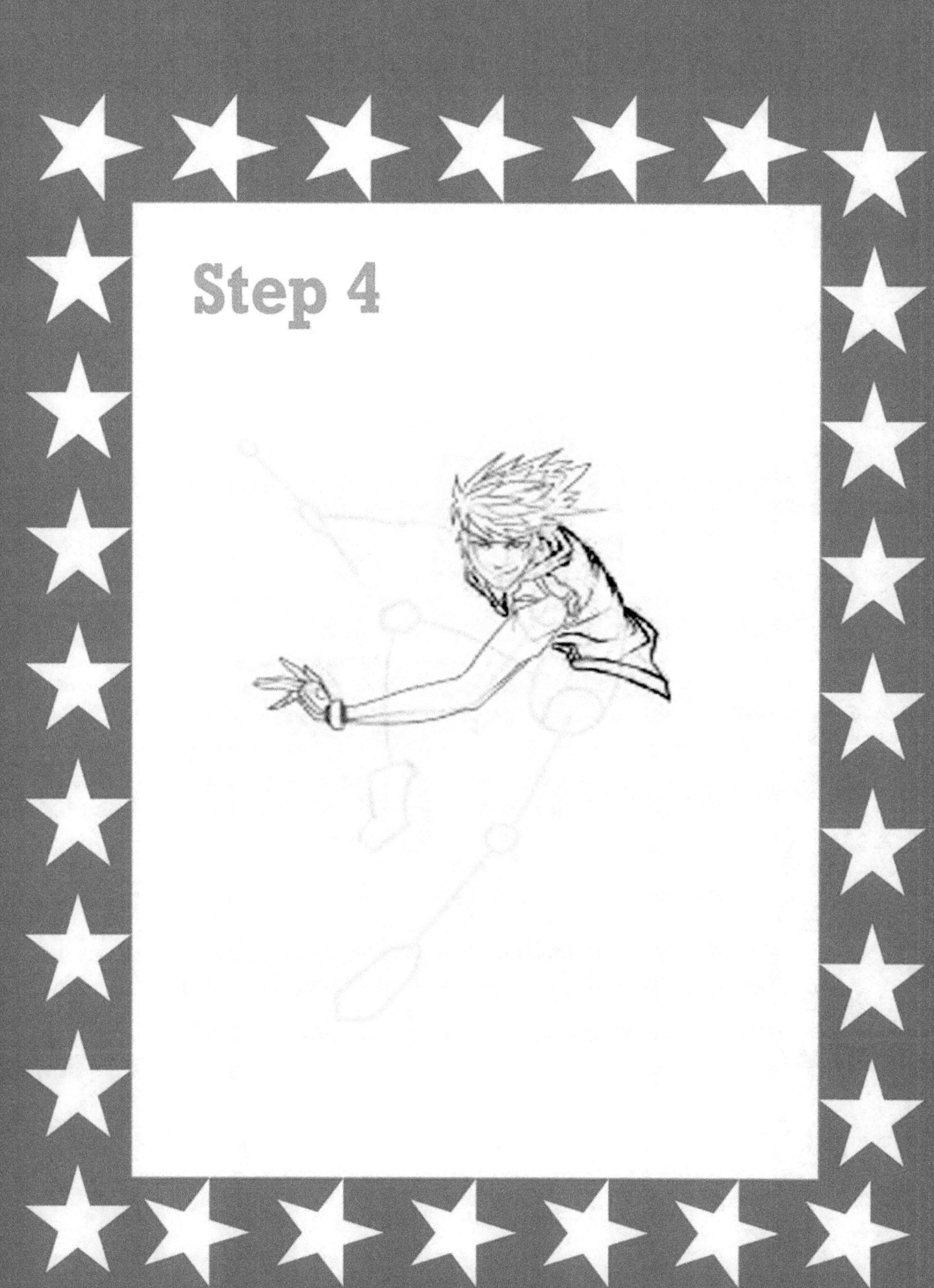

Step 5

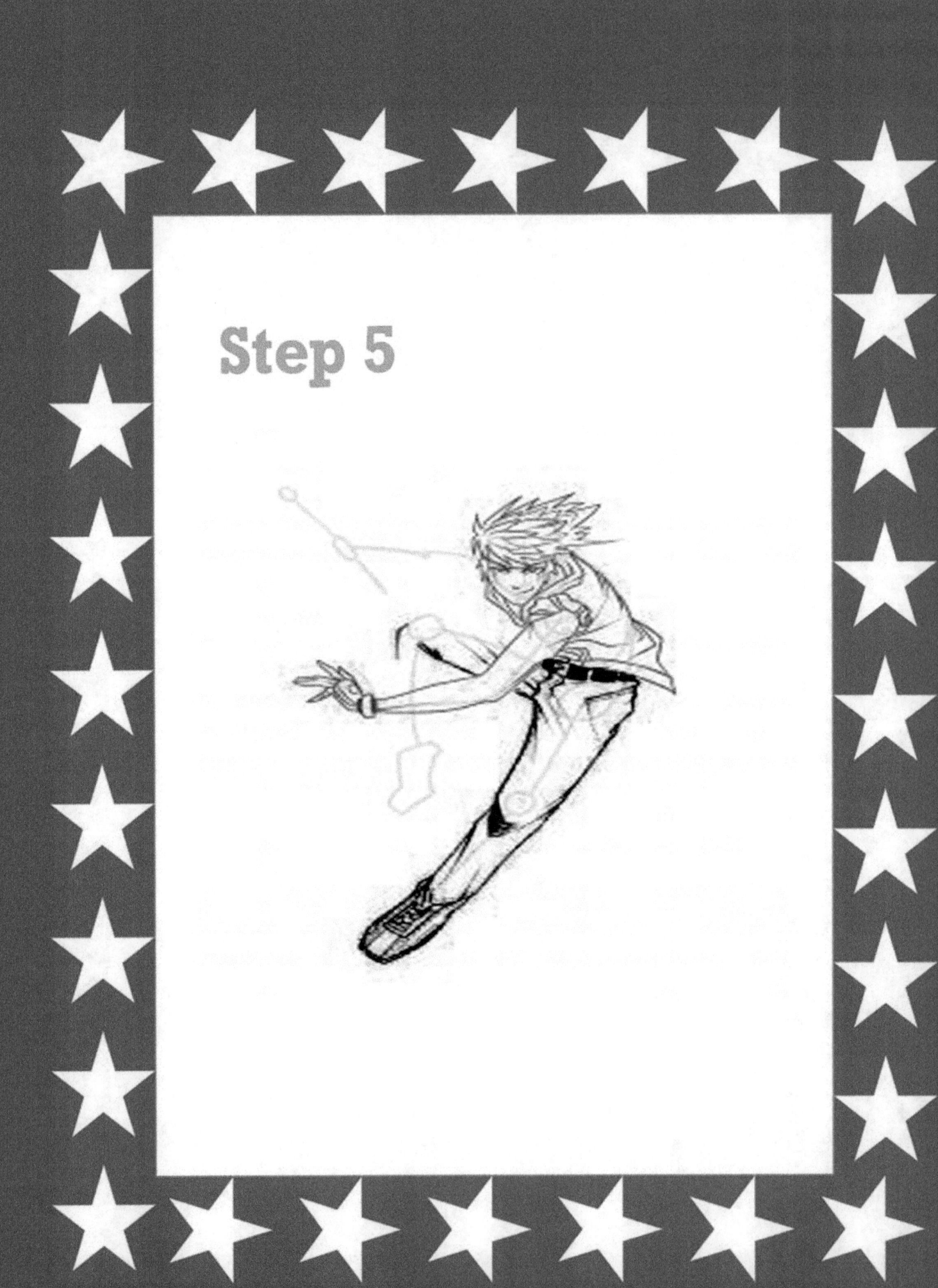

Step 6

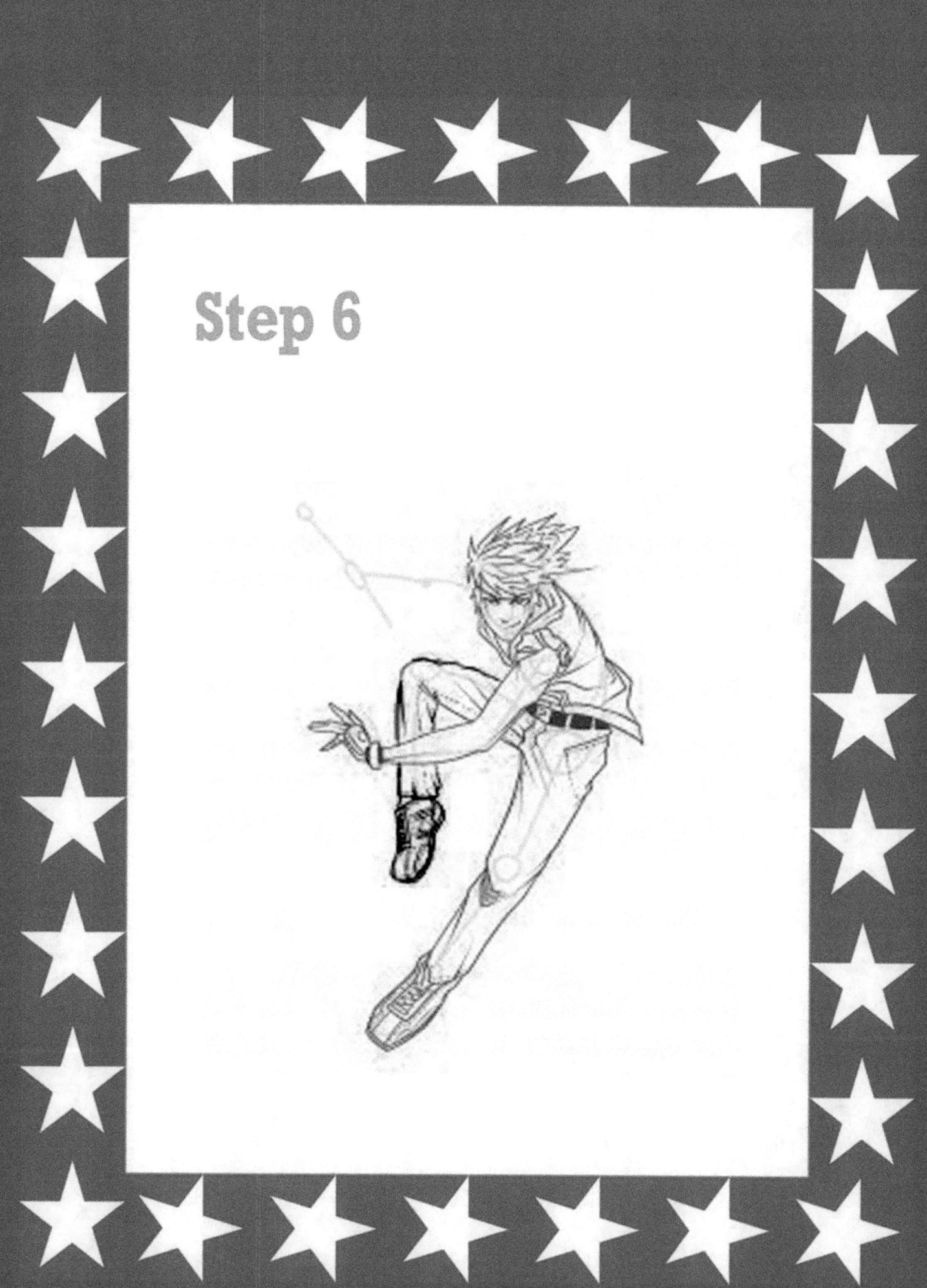

Step 7

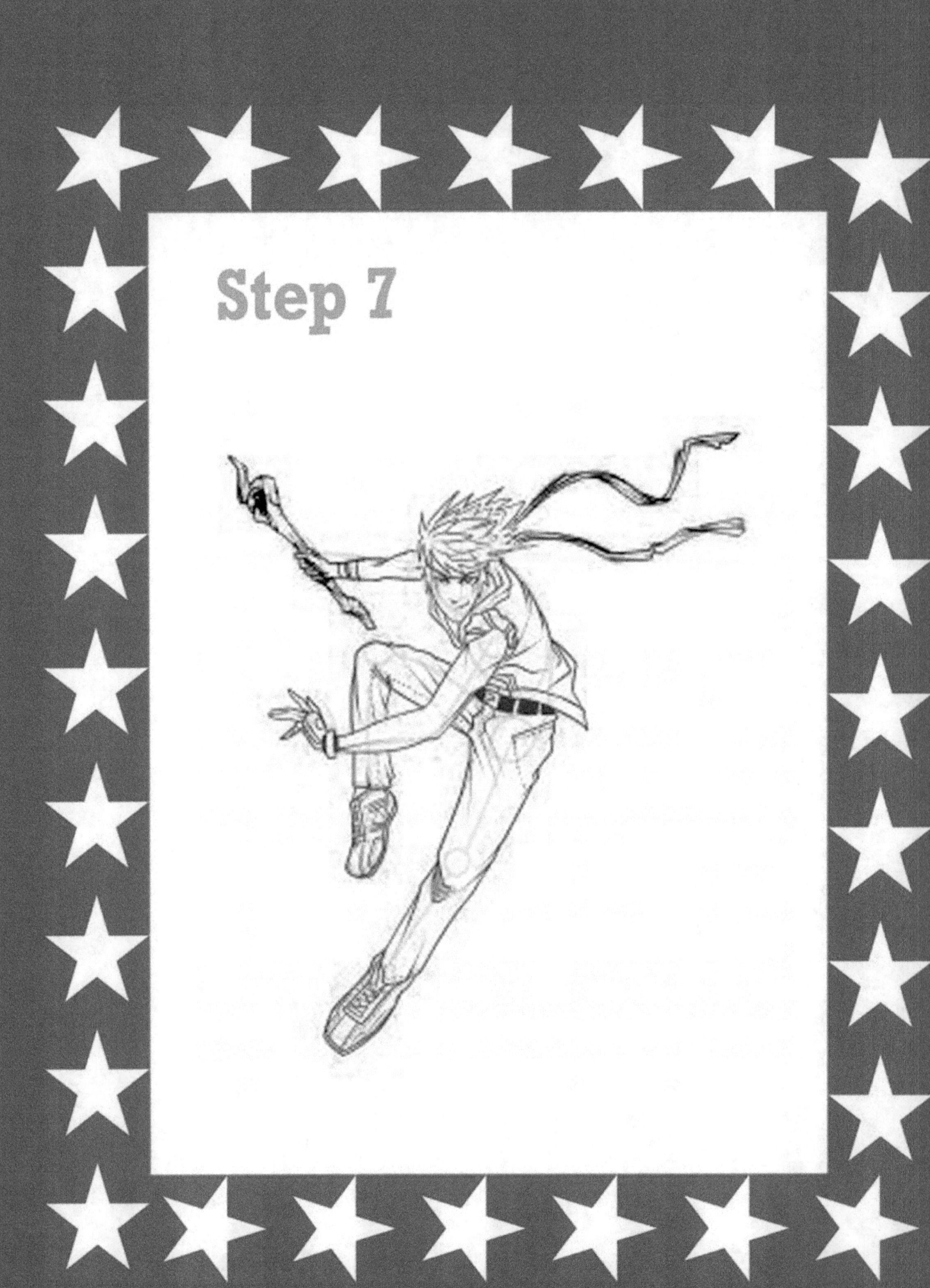

Step 8

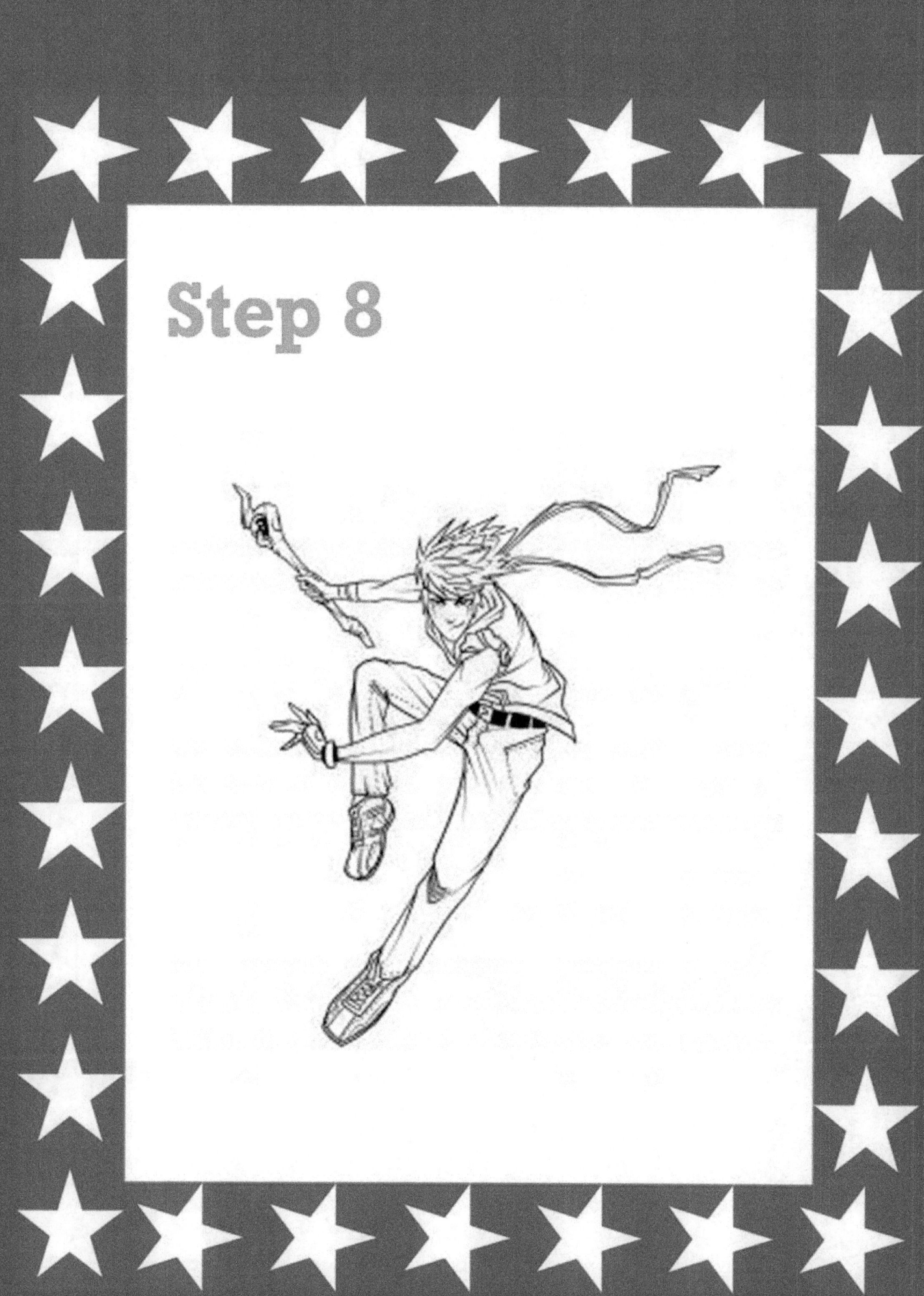

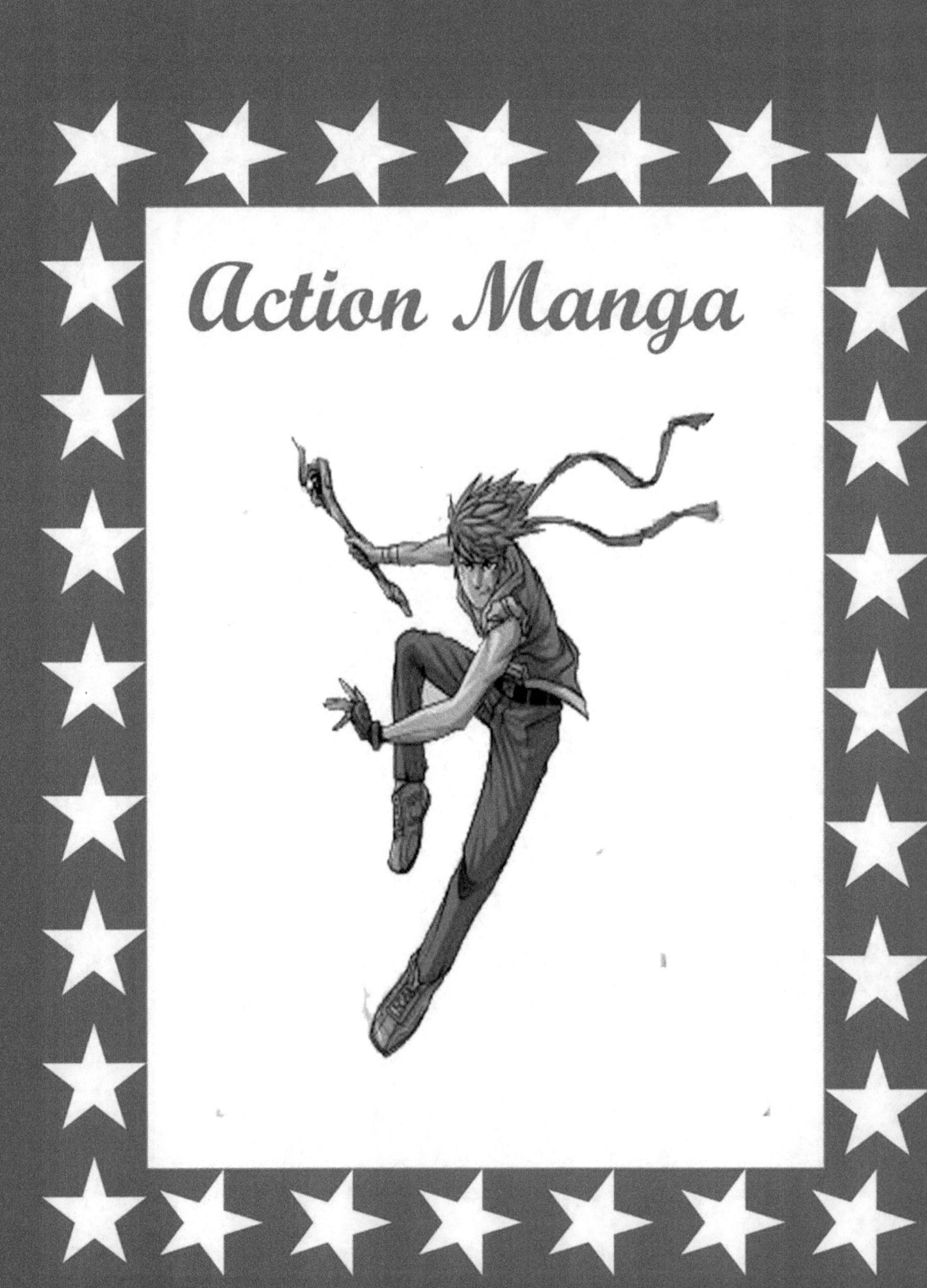

Step 1

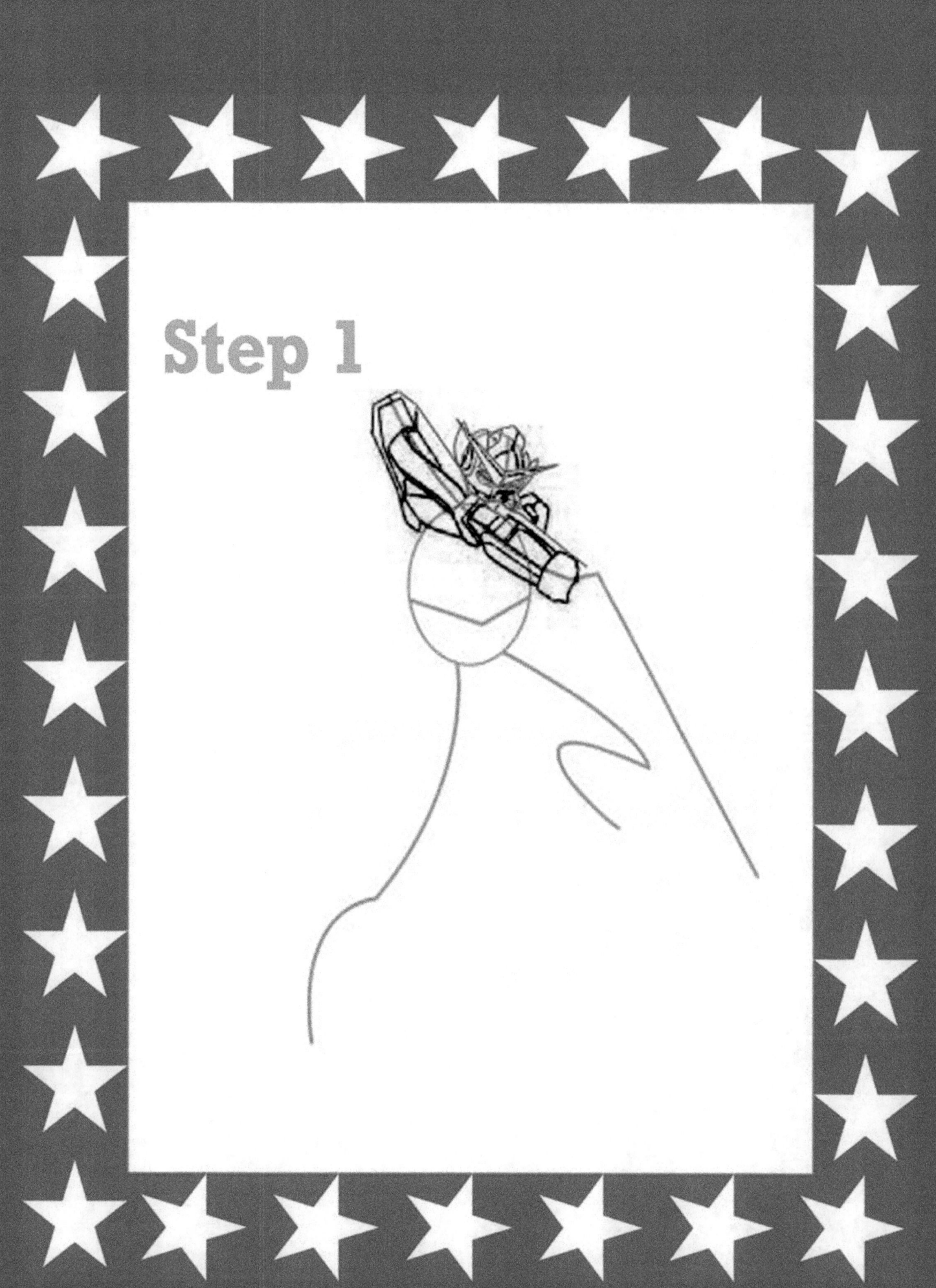

Step 2

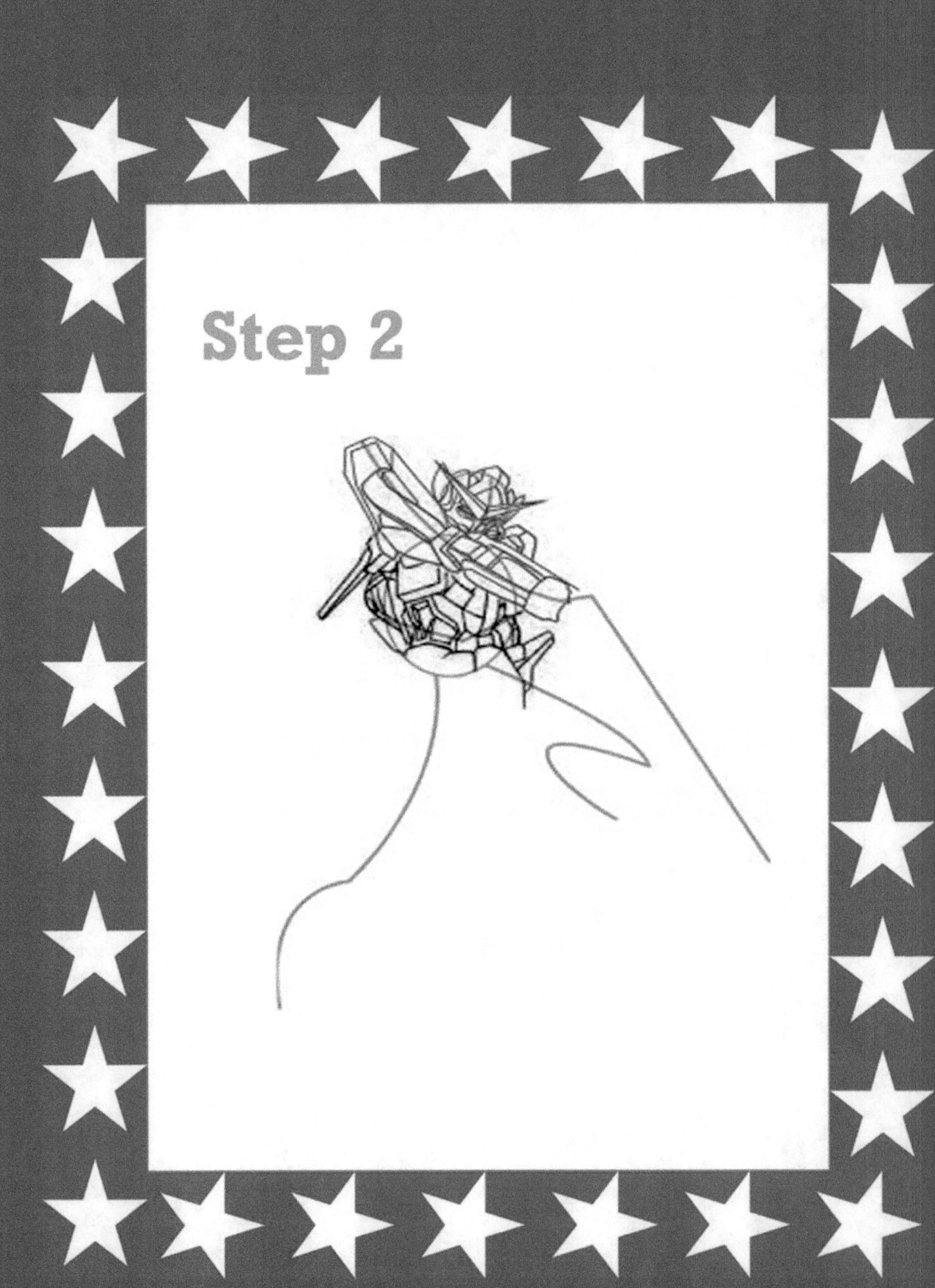

Step 3

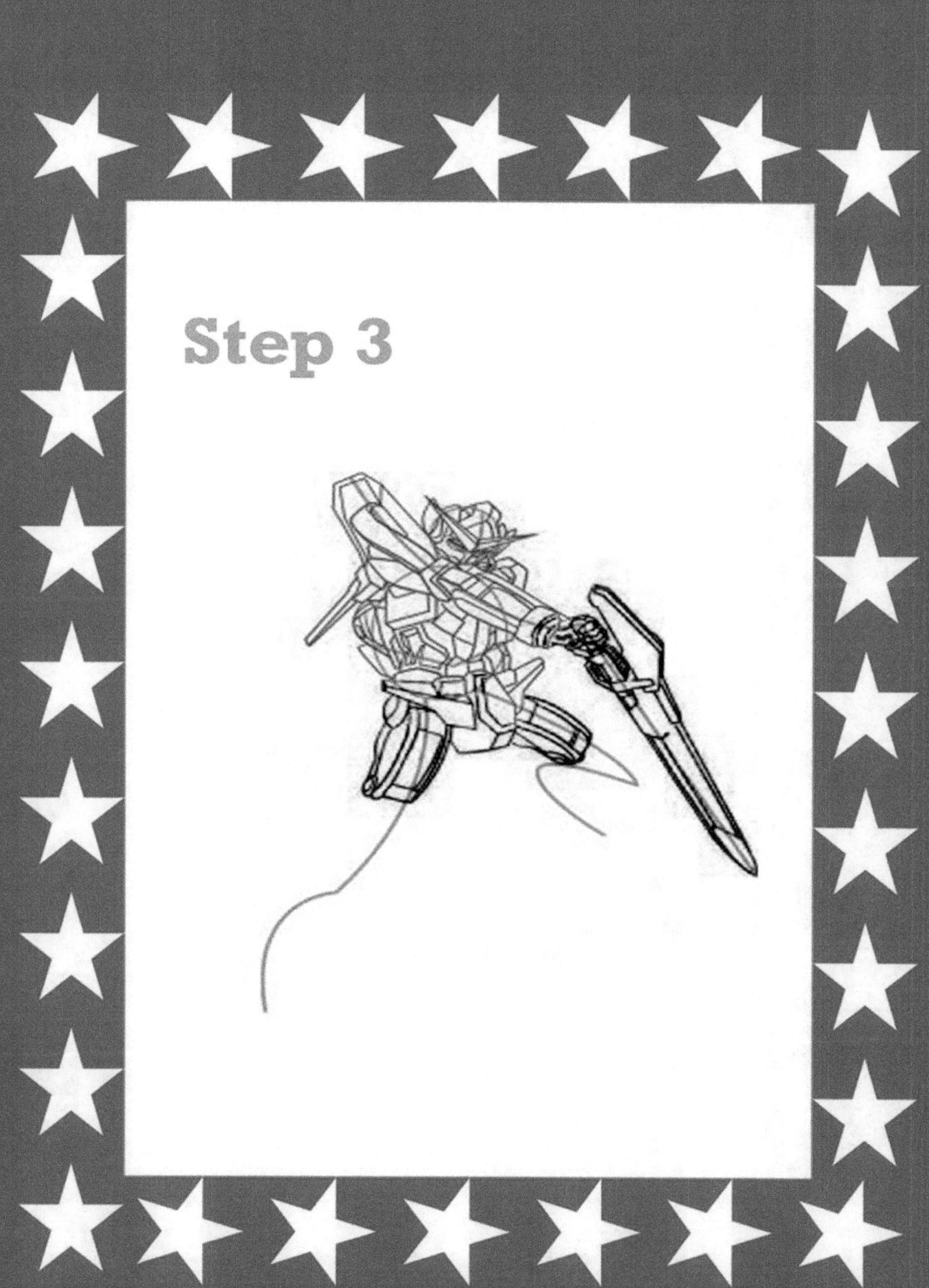

Step 4

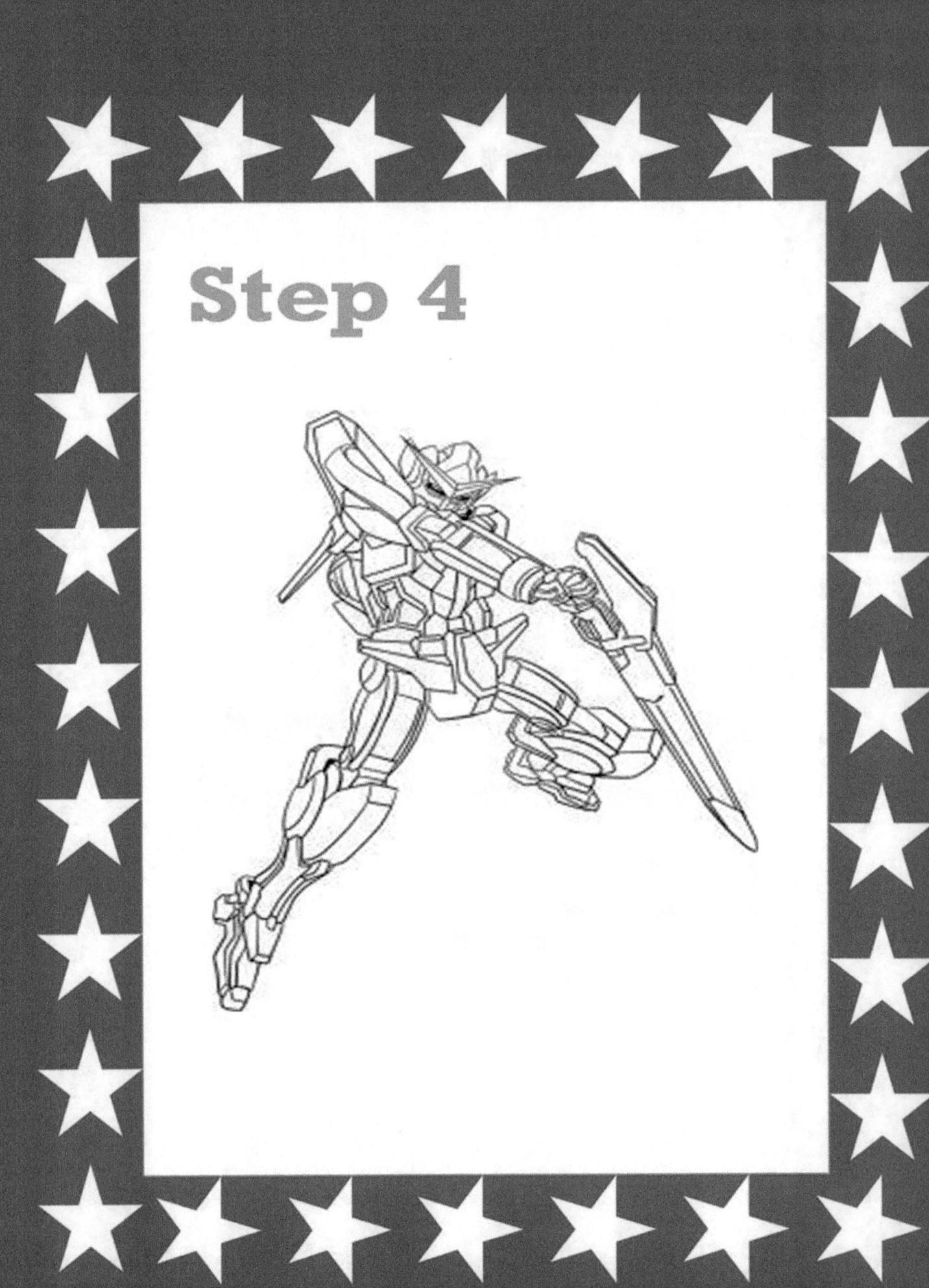

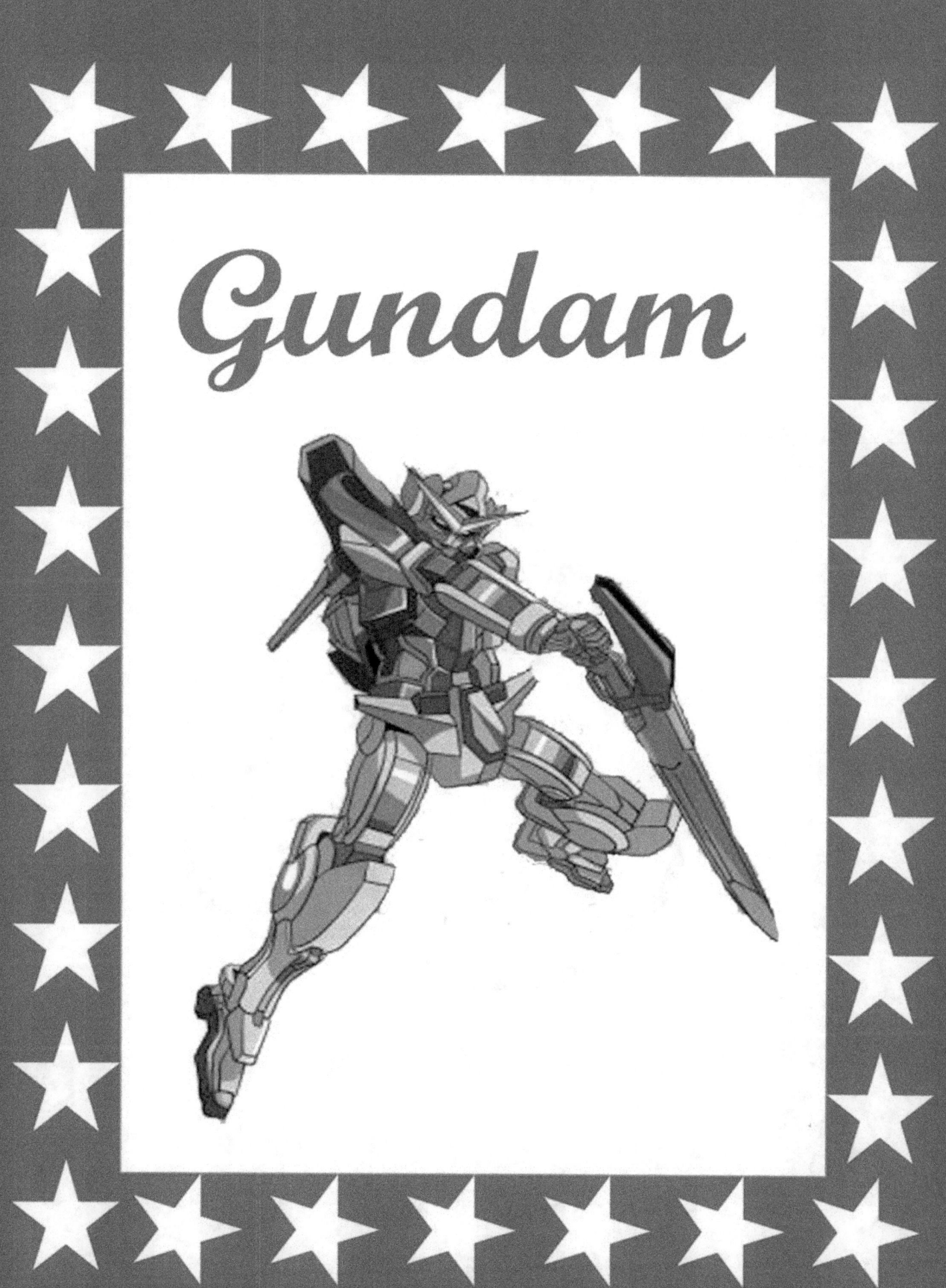

Step 1

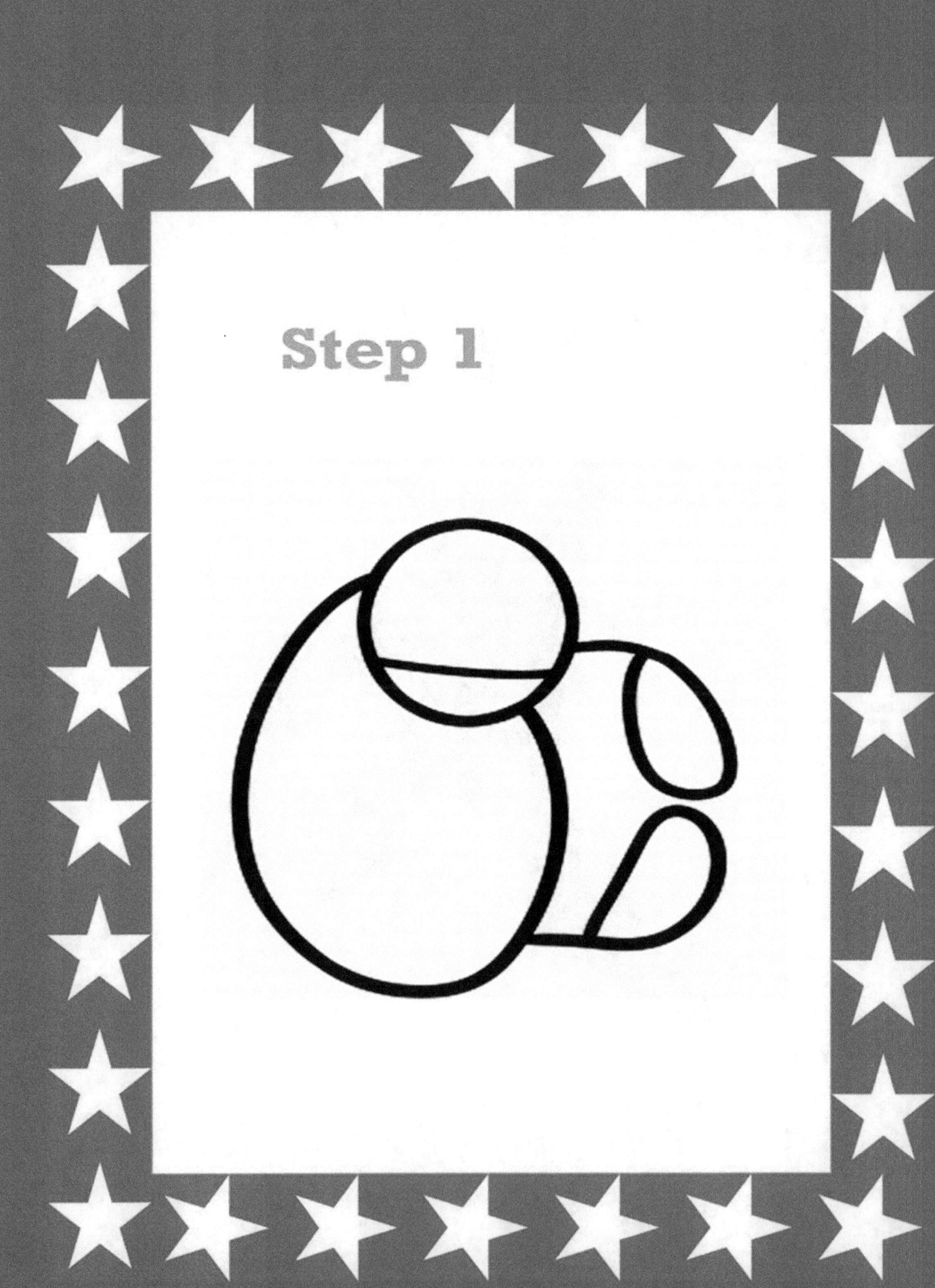

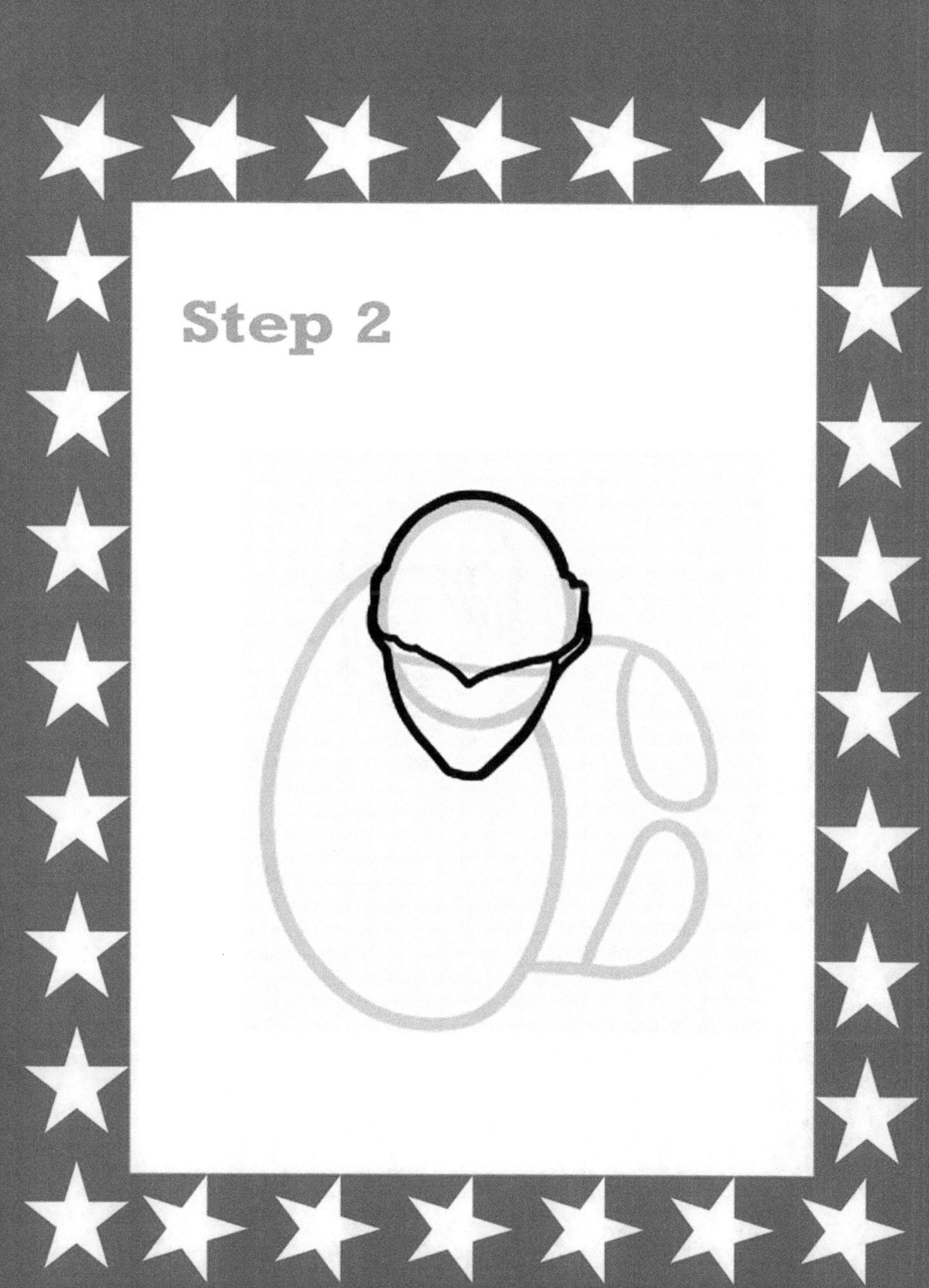

Step 2

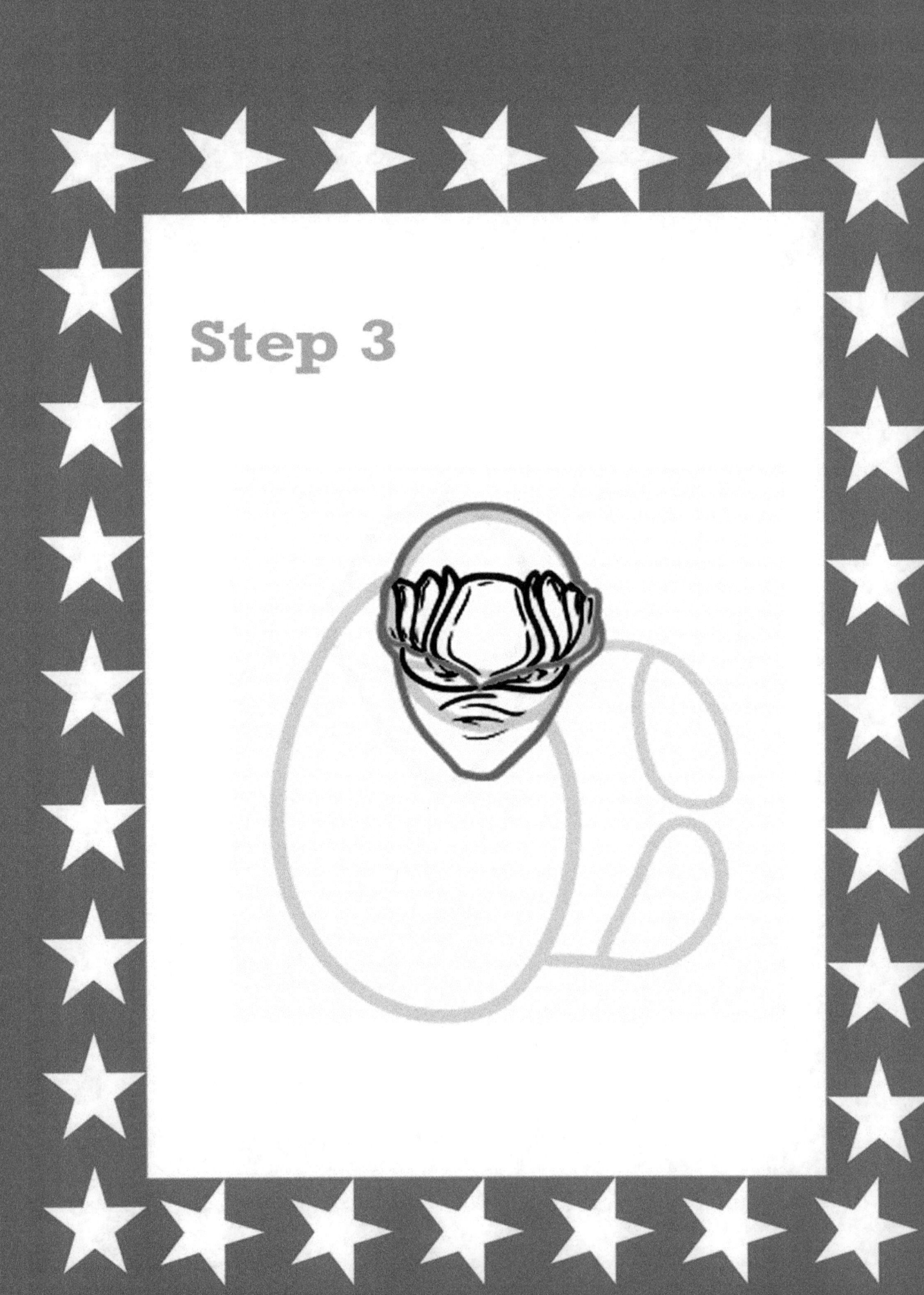

Step 3

Step 4

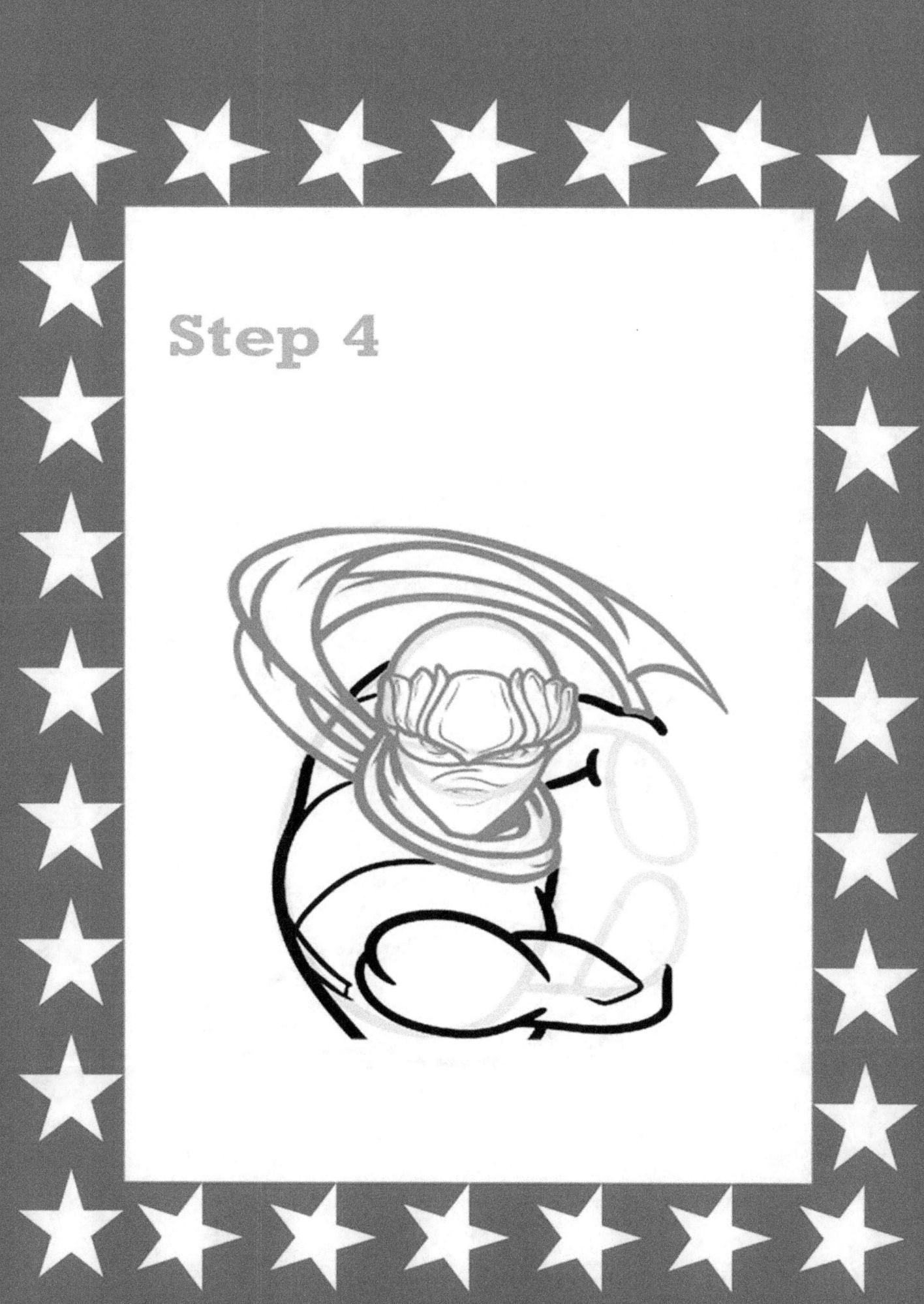

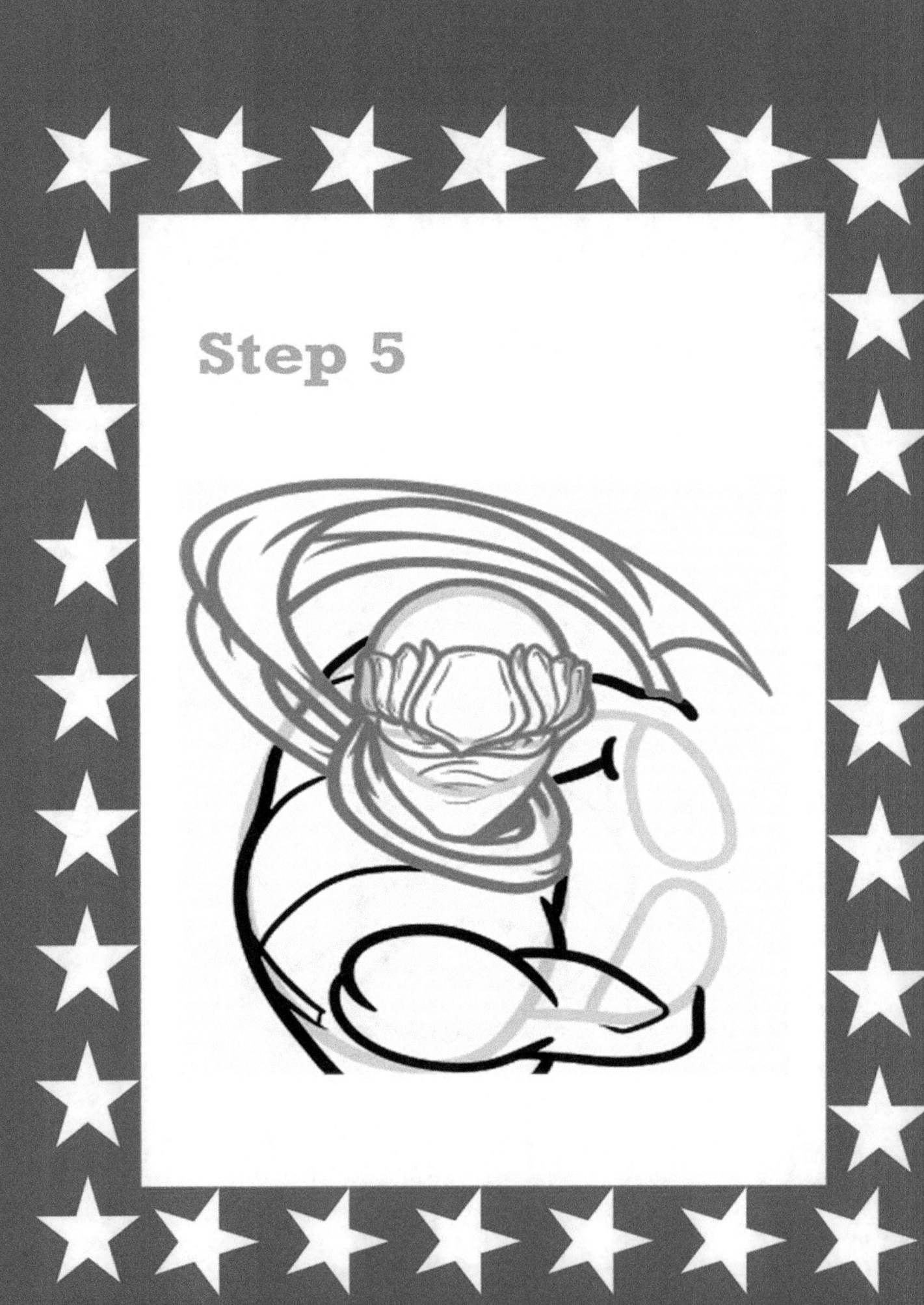

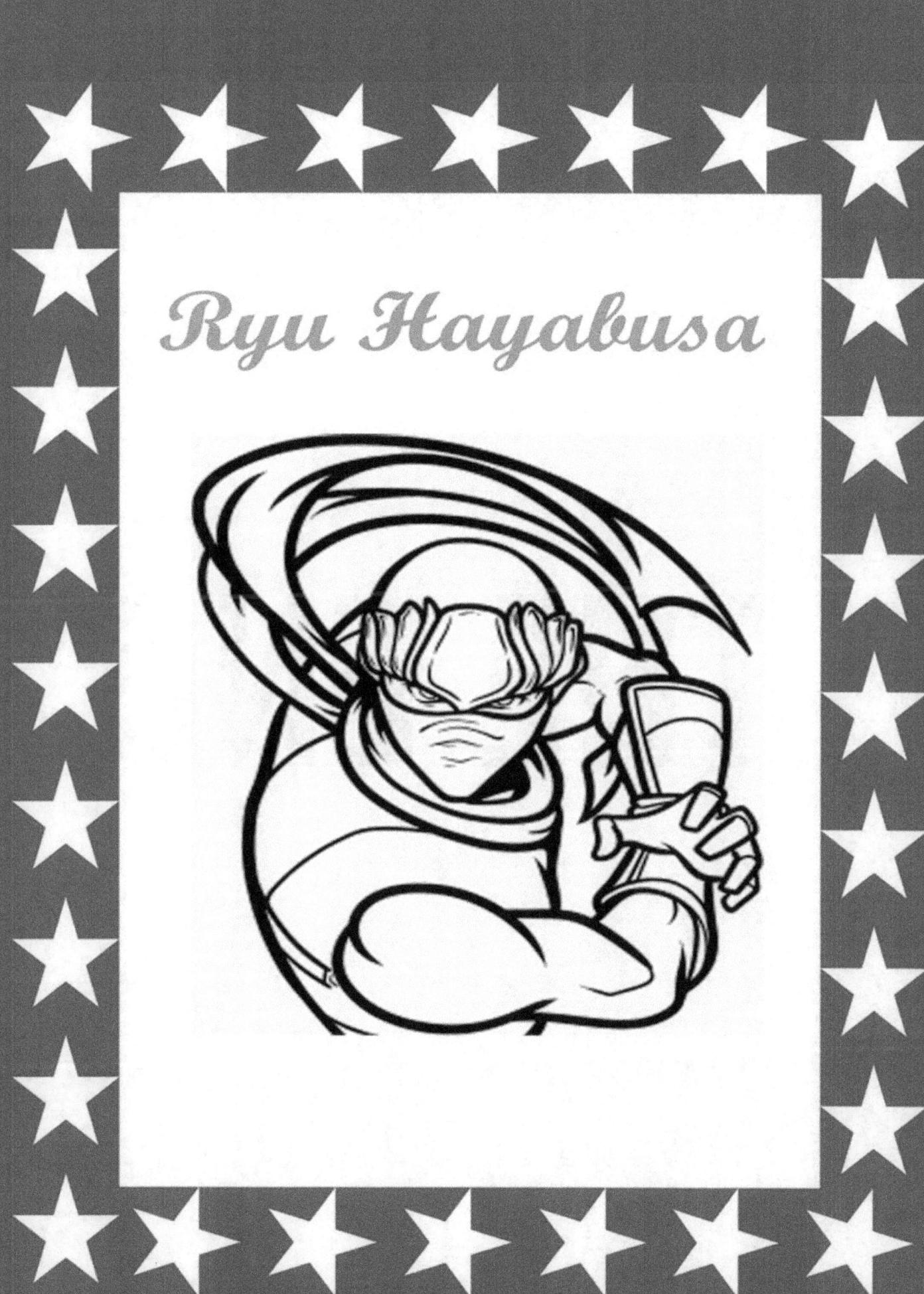

THE END

www.ingramcontent.com/pod-product-compliance
Lightning Source LLC
Chambersburg PA
CBHW080630180526
45168CB00007B/3116